In Case of Emergency

A Book for Computer Security Experts at the Edge of a Nervous

Breakdown

Aska

© Copyright Aska 2015

ISBN : 978-1-326-45938-3

All rights reserved.

Self published title.

Any reproduction, representation, use or modification is prohibited without permission from the author.

For A.W.

Thanks to I.K.

All these quotes were noted by the author. Some have been reformulated to synthetic purpose.

1. Technical beginning

«At what what stage are we on the round cables subject? »

What about the square ones?

« In case of massive network failure, we want to send a message to all customer devices indicating that there is a massive network failure. »

Yes, right on!.

« I do not think that the kernel is essential. »

That's why we call it "Kernel" by the way.

« Uh, you want to ensure compatibility with all OS? »

« Well, there are only two of them: Windows and Mac! »

Whew!

« That's not an API; an API is the thing we publish on our website. »

Complicated meeting.

« Remember the thing that only worked half the time? We received the fix: now it never works. »

Moving forward.

« We made a functional update without adding new functions. »

Convenient.

« We use a current date that changes constantly. »

The one that does not change is less useful.

« We'll spare you the list of bugs. »

Yes, please.

« We have instability: we must plug an Ethernet cable to make the Wi-Fi works. »

But after that part, it works!

« At one point in a project, when the code is mature, bugs arise: that is related to code maturity. »

It's well known.

« We have found a random source of bugs. »

That's not every day that you find a new entropy source.

« Now, we have to see how to handle the versioning of the version. »

Difficult subject.

« On these bugs, we have a good feeling. »

We are now reassured.

« To lower the error rate associated with this component, we propose to turn it on 65% of the time instead of 90%. »

Sure, it will reduce the error rate.

« Here, it's an average of three test results. »

That's relevant.

« We made a list of all necessary bugs. »

We should not forget to deploy those.

« When the debug traces are enabled, we no longer reproduce the bug. »

Very reassuring.

« We've just received the fix of the fix. »

Good.

« We have no more internet in the district because of a cable break, we are forced to use Wi-Fi to work. »

That's not how it works.

« Since it is so slow to boot from Flash, why don't we boot from RAM? »

Good idea! Get a patent!

« That's it! I understood the difference between smart card and SIM card: the SIM card lacks a corner! »

What if I started meditation? Oooohhm

« We are working on a new component, the Apeepee Shop. »

Also called Apeepee Store.

2. Project mode

« We were on mute, could you repeat the question? »

The mute for ears.

« I remain convinced that we are heading towards a controlled debacle. »

Ok then, let's go.

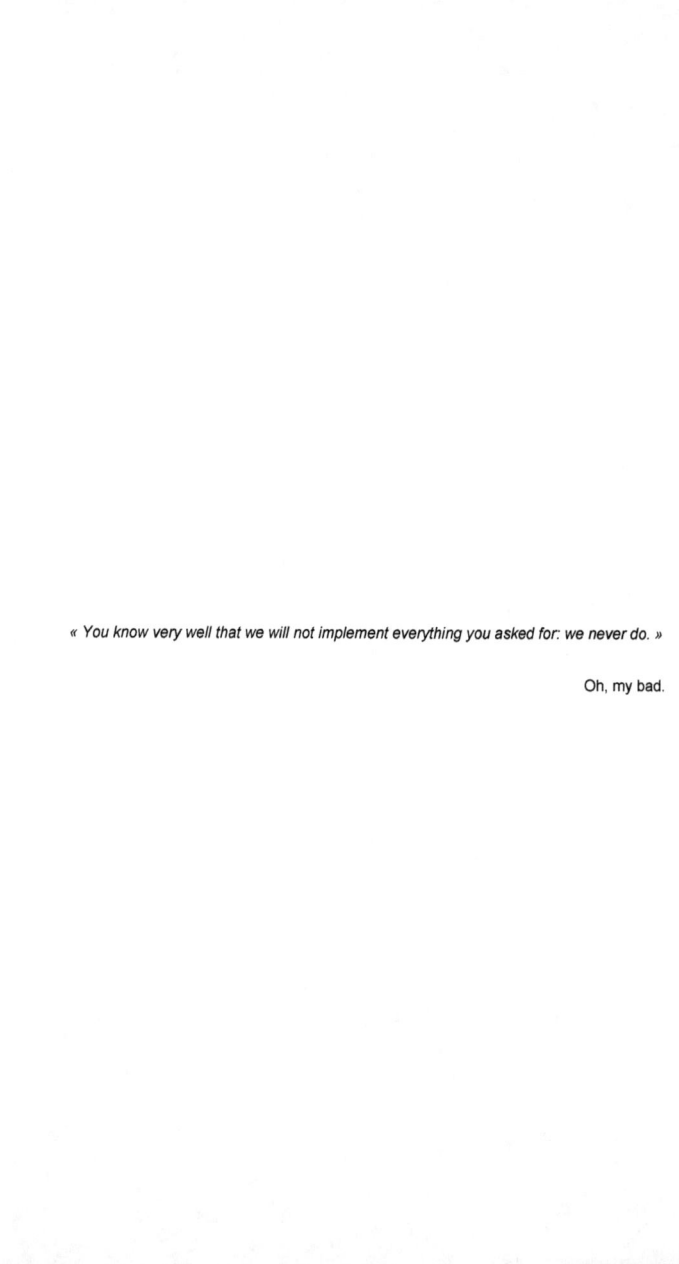

« You know very well that we will not implement everything you asked for: we never do. »

Oh, my bad.

« Your warnings are a bit disturbing, they scared the leaders. »

New concept: the reassuring warnings.

« You have to pay for bugs fixes: if you had not asked us new functions, there would have been no bug. »

Irrefutable.

« We're never late on delivering our sprints. We just don't do everything. »

Agile.

« On this schedule, nothing has changed except the dates. »

The date does not matter.

« We're late because of the Chinese New Year. »

On our side, it's because of Christmas.

« Ah, but this is a Friday subject! Today is Tuesday, that's why I did not understand. »

Process.

« It is better to write a slide full of crap than to do nothing. At least, it sets things. »

Now, we know what crap is.

« He is at the entrance of the door, he is coming. »

Is it painful?

« Because when there is a cat among the pigeons, it's not an electrician with crocodile clips that will help us»

No, it's not.

« We must glue back together the planets. »

So easy!

« There is a tree to build, and leafs to select. »

Okayyyyy.

« Today, the smoke is not so black. »

The glass is half full.

« We need managers in the case we need to cut our arms. »

Management.

« I've decided to make a meeting to get everyone together. »

Risky decision.

« Good news: we've identified forty blocking issues. »

Yeah !

« We will secure the issue. »

Otherwise, we could resolve it without meaning it.

« Efficacy has not enabled us to progress this week. »

Bad girl Efficacy ! Bad girl !

« It can change the course of time. »

Really?

« This is the problem with steps: if you put them under, you cannot put them above »

Logic.

« Would it not be better to do a realistic forecast? »

Are you crazy?

« There is also a third scenario, called 'scenario 4'. »

Microsoft did launch a trend.

3. Secured quotes

« There cannot be flaws: it is in JavaScript! »

An expert died during this meeting.

« It's not easy to do authentication. First of all: there is crypto in it. »

Indeed.

« The fact that the password is generated from data known by the attacker is not a problem, he still needs to know who owns which password. »

A fellow expert, I think.

« You do not really want us to follow all CVEs applying to our product, do you? »

Yes, we do.

« This is the problem with risks, you can never be sure. »

Maybe we could use reassuring warnings?

« 'Encrypt', this is ok, I understand, 'Signed' also. But 'secured', I don't understand. »

The worst is: it actually makes sense.

« The format of the certificate does not follow the standard, but there's no impact: the server does not check it anyway. »

Everything's good.

« Non-compliance: password not encrypted in flows N° X / Y / Z. But that's a standard issue. »

So, no problem!

« Your security patch PaX kills our driver due to a memory corruption. Please, remove the security patch. »

It's not a bug, it's a feature.

« When writing an input longer than expected in that field, it overwrites adjacent memory data. Fortunately we have one version where the input is shorter, we will deploy this one. »

Perfect.

« We do not need to protect ourselves from hardware level attacks. If the user opens his product, he loses the warranty anyway. »

We all know how much attackers love their warranties.

« What do you think about putting the SSO in the Big Data? »

Buzz-words.

« We do not find the DES in your crypto algorithms recommendation. »

2015

« We do not think that the real problem is that all processes run as root. »

We still don't know what the 'real' problem is.

« Indeed, the RAM spaces are never write + executable simultaneously. Unless requested by an ELF, of course. »

Don't kill anybody.

« We don't need to password protect the Wi-Fi: the attacker still needs to be in our offices, and we will know that he does not belong here. »

Absolute security measure.

« Even if it's online, this server URL cannot be browse. »

Untouchable server.

« The hypervisor, do you put it up or down in your model? »

We put it near the supervisor.

« We don't risk a thing: it's in the LAN. »

Why is everyone concerned about this?

« For better security, we put the LDAP server offline. That way, the attacker cannot even retrieve public keys. »

The best is the enemy of the good.

« I do not think that elliptic curves are more secure than RSA. Finding 2048 bits by brute force is way more complicated than 256! »

It is worth publishing.

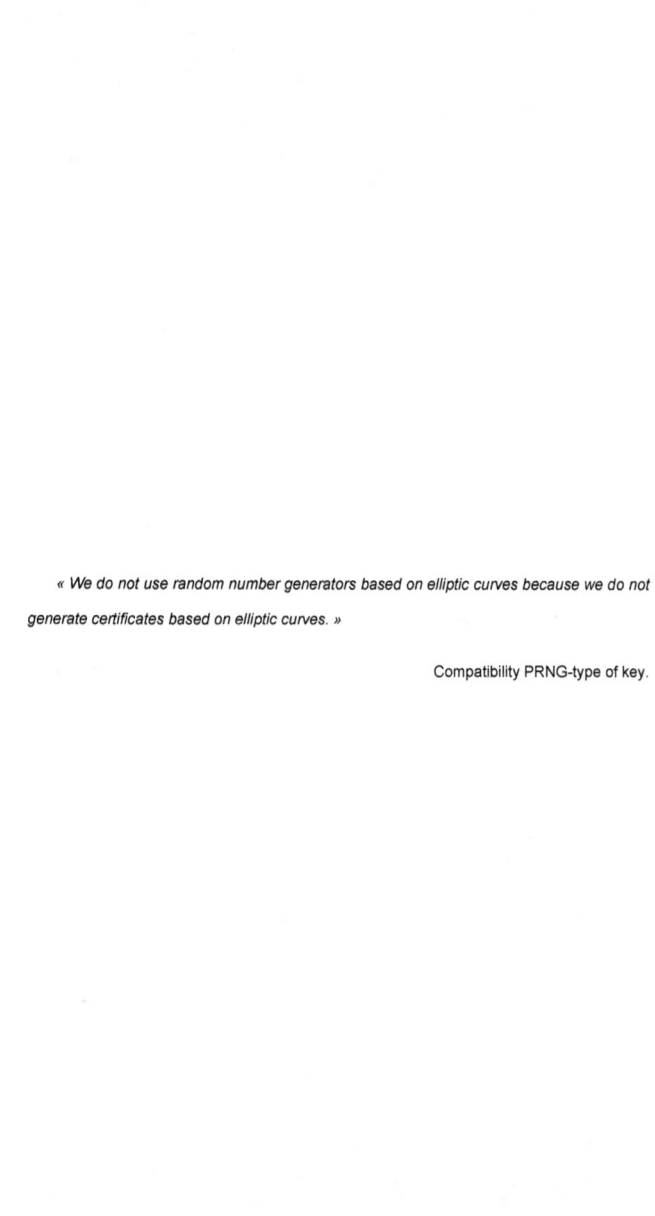

« We do not use random number generators based on elliptic curves because we do not generate certificates based on elliptic curves. »

Compatibility PRNG-type of key.

« I'm watching from time to time the generator output: if it does not look random, I throw away the file. »

Organizational measure.

« Our password is chosen randomly, but not in the cryptographic sense: we choose one to which an attacker would not think first. »

The generation process must be interesting.

« Security flaws, functional regression: please, do not play with words! »

All the same.

« Please, indicate a percentage of completion for your security audit »

To use: (number of days spent on the audit x 100) / number of days provided for the audit.

« You keep talking about those Russian hackers. But we don't sell our product in Russia! »

No way they can get one.

« The file is signed with MD5. »

Nooooooo

« We have an ergonomic issue: the application asks the user his password. We propose to use a simple password for this service, common to all users, so that the application doesn't need to ask it to the user. »

You are missing a point here.

« I've noticed that you often make the same mistake on your slides: its KPI not PKI. »

Key Performance Indicator.

« The teenager is not going to reboot the product just to bypass the parental control! »

Naive much?

« That's not a personal data; this is just the user profile picture! »

Nothing personal.

« The string used by the auditor for his XSS attack is now banned. »

That's the way to do it!

4. What about the author?

« You saw Goldeneye? When it takes two people who turn two keys simultaneously to launch a missile? Well, a key ceremony is the same, but instead of launching a missile you generate a certificate authority. »

Key ceremonies are so sexy.

« A certificate signed by a recognized trusted authority is like a passport. A certificate signed by an unrecognized authority is like your credit card: not easy to falsify, but it is not recognized as proof of identity by the State. A self-signed certificate is like your swimming club card, easy to falsify, but hey, it's for the pool. »

They did get it!

« Electronic signature is like a post-it. »

Do think about it.

To be continued ...

www.ingramcontent.com/pod-product-compliance
Lightning Source LLC
Chambersburg PA
CBHW070426180526
45158CB00017B/811